The Offering

That Breaks The Curse

BISHOP DR. DEXTER JAMES

Dexter James Impartation Ministry
Email: thewealthambassador@hotmail.com
Telephone: 1-868-289-4325

All scripture quotations are taken from the King James Version of the Bible unless otherwise stated.

ISBN: 978-1-7351512-2-9

Printed in Trinidad and Tobago

My purpose for writing this book is to help people in the area of their finances, by showing them the difference between a curse and a blessing. I will also explain how to break the curse of lack and poverty and step into more than enough. You got something in your life right now, right at this moment that will create the future you desire, if only you know what to do with it, your life will change for the better.

Prayer Before Reading This Book

Heavenly Father I thank You for your anointing, for Your power that is going to enable me to understand what I am reading so that I can develop, act and get the results that I need to get in Jesus name Amen.

Contents

CHAPTER ONE

WHAT DOES IT MEAN TO BE CURSED

Many people in the body of Christ are not aware of the power or the force of a curse. I must admit to you I was ignorant of it to a certain extent until December 31st 2009 when I was preaching on a subject, "It has to end before 2010." During my message the Lord began to reveal to me what really happens when someone is cursed and I will reveal some of those things that happen to people when they are dealing with a curse.

I would like you to understand when a curse is working nothing you do will work for good. Everything works against you when a curse is working. Now please note I am not saying everything that is not working is a curse in operation. It will take spiritual discernment, wise counsel and mentorship to let you know the difference between a natural problem and a spiritual problem (a curse). We will look at some scriptures that speak about curses and see what happens when someone is curse.

Deuteronomy 28:15 , "But it shall come to pass, if thou wilt not hearken unto the voice of the Lord thy God, to observe to do all his commandments and his statutes which I command thee this day; that all these curses shall come upon thee, and overtake thee."

Before we go any further I want you to know that God is talking to the Israelites and He is telling them that curses will come upon them if they do not obey His commandments. I want you to know that there are Christians who are redeemed from the curse that has allowed them to keep living under the curse because of wrong decisions.

Let us continue in Deuteronomy and look at some curses, its effects and the area of our lives its affects.

Curse # 1

Deuteronomy 28:16, "Cursed shalt thou be in the city."

This is what the word of God is saying, "cursed shall thou be in the city." Please note the curse affects what happens in the city to the individual that it is connected to. Whenever that individual is in a city, there is no favor, no opportunity, nothing works for them, their business is not making money, they are losing money daily, and customers are not buying as they should in-spite of all their marketing strategies. Most people may think things like these are normal but it is not, especially if it is happening constant. What is happening in cases like these is a curse at work that needs to be stopped.

Curse # 2

Deuteronomy 28:16 Cursed shalt thou be in field.

When you are cursed in the field it means that nothing you do in field will be productive. For example, let's say for the past three years 2007, 2008 and 2009 you have planted corn but every time you were about to harvest your corn a storm or flood will come and destroy it. That is not normal; it is a curse at work that needs to be stopped.

Curse # 3

Deuteronomy 28:17 Cursed shall be thy basket and thy store.

When your basket and store is curse that mean you cannot save anything, you cannot keep anything but you keep having need of everything.

Curse # 4

Deuteronomy 28:18, "Cursed shall be the fruit of thy body."

The fruit of your body speaks of your children. This curse is the reason for constant miscarriages sometimes. This curse is the reason sometimes for your children constantly going to jail. This curse is the reason sometimes for your children's broken marriages and the list can go on and on.

Curse # 5

Deuteronomy 28:18, "Cursed shall be the fruit of thy land."

When your land is cursed nothing grows, nothing produce, nothing happens to your seed.

I believe many in the body of Christ are struggling and are living unproductive lives because they are not where God wants them to be. It is possible to do the right thing in the wrong place. Doing the right thing in the wrong place will never produce results, for example apple seeds were designed to be sown in the earth, grow and produce, but if you plant apples here in Trinidad they would not grow. They were not designed to grow in this kind of climate or environment.

Curse # 6

Deuteronomy 28:18, "Cursed shall be the increase of thy kine and the flocks of thy sheep.

When the increase of your animals is cursed that means some of your animals that are born die before you can benefit from it or someone may steal it.

Curse # 7

Deuteronomy 28:19, "Cursed shalt thou be when thou comest in and cursed shalt thou be when thou goest out.

When you're coming in, and you're going out, and the curse is working that means your journey is curse. If your journey is cursed that means there is no progress in your life but only constant disappointment.

Curse # 8

Deuteronomy 28:20, " The Lord shall send upon thee cursing, vexation, and rebuke, in all that thou settest thine hand unto for to do, until thou be destroyed, and until thou be destroyed, and until thou perish quickly."

Decrease, lack, poverty and not moving forward are signs of a curse at work that need to be stopped.

After looking at these scriptures we see that as believers we need to get in line with God and his word if we have to live curse free lives. If you study Deuteronomy chapter twenty eight, (Deut 28) starting from the fifteen verse (v.15), you will notice that the curse came by a decision. Now if the curse came by a decision then the curse can be stopped by a decision.

In Deuteronomy 30:19, the scripture says, "I call heaven and earth to record this day against you, that I have set before you life and death, blessing and cursing: therefore choose life that both thou and thy seed may live."

I would like you to understand that one curse working against you can kill your future. A curse has a killer nature; it is assigned to you, to stop your future, so you cannot go forward, so you cannot advance. That is why you better stop it, before it stops you.

As a child of God you must understand that a curse is not a blessing from God or a gift from Him. It is what it is, a curse and it needs to be broken. When a curse is at work you will be blocked off from increase, multiplication, overflow, abundance, plenty and more than enough.

It does not matter what you do, when the curse is working nothing increases for your good. I know many believers will say there is no curse working against them, but let me ask you a question, what have you been able to accomplish for the Lord with great significance, that makes the ungodly and even some believers wonder what had happened? What have you accomplished in your personal life that only God's grace on your life could allow you to accomplish it? If you are unable to produce that evidence, there is curse working.

A curse is a spirit that is assigned to cause you harm, to stop your fruitfulness, to stop you from flourishing, to stop you from blossoming, to stop you from rising up, to stop you from going forward, to stop you from progressing, to stop you from advancing. I believe that sometimes a curse can be released on your life through the spirit of heaviness. That makes it hard for you to act or make the right move.

When a curse is at work it does not matter how well you can do something, others will rise above you, and others will be seen quicker than you. When a curse is at work it literally paralyzes your future, it freezes you.

The curse can bring you to a position where you are no different than a statue in other words you cannot move.

That which is assigned (the curse) to stop you, needs to be stopped now in Jesus name.

The curse needs to be stopped before it stops you, now in Jesus name. Amen.

CHAPTER TWO

CAN SOMEONE CURSE ME?

Yes someone can curse you. But for someone to curse you it is not easy as some people think and it is not as hard as some people think. Now let me explain firstly what I mean by not so easy as some people think. When you are living for God and His blessing is upon you, no man can curse you, it does matter how hard they try. Once you stand your ground and stay in the blessing circle no curse will be able to work against you. Let us look at this scripture.

Numbers 22: 12, "And God said unto Balaam, thou shalt not go with them; thou shalt not curse the people: for they are blessed."

Because the children of Israel were blessed, Balaam could not curse them once they were in right standing with God. Now if you read the verses before, you will see why Balak wanted to curse them, it is because he wanted to stop them from increasing, from multiplying and expanding. But if you notice, he could not stop them because the blessing was working for the children of Israel it was upon them. So he decided to call someone to curse them because he know from the time the children of Israel get curse he can take over, he can stop them from expanding and stop them from increasing. And that is what the devil is doing to some of God's people, keep them cursed by allowing them to refuse to pay their tithes and give offerings. Also by using believers to fight biblical prosperity so he can stop the kingdom from expanding, so he can stop the church from increasing. I want to make a statement, the devil is smarter than some Christians when it comes to money because he knows if he can keep the curse of poverty working against the believer he knows, not to long from now we will not be able to reach the lost as we should. As children of God, always remember this, it cost to reach the lost.

In this verse we see that Balaam was unable to curse God's people because of the blessing. In verse eighteen (v.18) this what the scriptures says;

"And Balaam answered and said unto the servants of Balak, if Balak would give me his house full of silver and gold, I cannot go beyond the word of the Lord my God, to do less or more."

As a child of God once God has blessed you and you stay in covenant relationship with Him no one will be able to curse you, it does not matter what they try.

Now let us look at how someone can curse you.

Numbers 23: 20-21, "Behold, I have received commandment to bless: and he hath blessed; and I cannot reverse it. He hath not beheld iniquity in Jacob, neither hath he seen perverseness in Israel: the Lord his God is with him, and the shout of a king is among them."

In verse twenty-one (v.21) of chapter twenty three (chpt 23), the Bible says that He, speaking of God, hath not beheld iniquity in Jacob, neither hath he seen perverseness in Israel: the Lord his God is with him and the shout of a king is among them. Now the reason why verse twenty (v.20) was working in their lives was because verse twenty-one (v.21) was working.

What Balaam was saying in other words, because the people are in right standing with God I cannot curse them? Once God's people are in right standing with Him, they cannot be cursed. The opposite is also true, once they are not in right standing with Him someone can pronounce a curse and it will take effective and stop them from moving forward. Child of God one bad rumour about you, your product, your company, your job performance or your character and as we will say in lay man terms all hell break loose. And because of those negative remarks, all of a sudden everything good in your life shut down and you cannot come out, all the negative things I listed above are curses that need to be stop. That is why the Bible told us in the latter part of Isaiah 54:17; "and every evil tongue that shall rise up against thee in judgment thou shalt condemn."

There are evil tongues and evil words that need to be condemned; they need to be stopped in Jesus name. Amen.

Proverbs 11:26, "He that withholdeth corn, the people shall curse him."

Yes someone can curse you if you are not position right.

The curse needs to be stopped before it stops you, now in Jesus name. Amen

CHAPTER THREE

CAN I CURSE MYSELF?

Yes you can curse yourself and we are going to let the scriptures speak.

Deuteronomy 28:15, "But it shall come to pass, if thou wilt not hearken unto the voice of the Lord thy God, to observe to do all his commandments and his statutes which I command thee this day; that all these curses shall come upon thee, and overtake thee."

Whenever the Lord gave you a command and you refuse to observe it, obey it and do it. You are literally positioning yourself to be cursed.

Malachi 3:6-9, "For I am the Lord, I change not; therefore ye sons of Jacob are not consumed. Even from the days of your fathers ye are gone away from mine ordinances, and not kept them. Return unto me, and I will return unto you, saith the Lord of hosts. But ye said, wherein shall we return?"

"Will a man rob God? Yet ye have robbed me. But ye say, wherein have we robbed thee in tithes and offerings? Ye are cursed with a curse: for ye have robbed me, even this whole nation." In this scripture we see where the children of Israel, God chosen people refuse to bring their tithes into the store house and they invoke a double curse on their lives. This is what the word says; "you are cursed with a curse." Now I know many none tithers who look like they a prospering financially, but there are many other challenges in their lives that they cannot solve because it will take more than money to deal with it. A Christian who refuses to pay tithes and consistently refuses to give offerings has curse themselves base on this scripture we have just look at.

Deuteronomy 30:19, "I call heaven and earth to record this day against you, that I have set before you life and death, blessing and cursing: therefore choose life, that both thou and thy seed may live."

There are two things set before you and that is blessing and cursing. It is set before you, so that you can choose. I have a question for you, what is your choice blessing or cursing. I hope you choose life (the blessing) because it is God's desire that you choose blessing.

Yes you can curse yourself and that is by the decision or decisions you choose to make. Isaiah 1:19, "says if ye be willing and obedient, ye shall eat the good of the land." But he did not stop there, in verse twenty, he said, but if ye refuse and rebel, ye shall be devoured with the sword: for the mouth of the Lord hath spoken it.

The prophet Isaiah let us know eating the good of land which speaks about blessing is based on our decision to obey the Lord. And to receive the opposite, which is to be devoured by the sword which is the curse at work. It will be based on your decision to rebel against God.

The curse needs to be stopped before it stops you, now in Jesus name.

CHAPTER FOUR

GOD'S ANSWER TO THE CURSE

We are about to go into a level of seed sowing that is about to make the devil and all his poverty demons call an emergency meeting, to announce that somebody is revealing what he have hidden from the church to keep them poor in evangelism and poor in outreach ministry. The day has come for a financial showdown and a financial showing up and showing off. The devil's financial system and strongholds in the minds of God's people are coming down in Jesus name.

Just like in the book of revelation that says the devil knows that he has a short time. The devil knows that he only have a short time with all the money that has been in the wicked hands and that is his reason for advancing in the area of evil so quick. Because he knows that assignment money, mission money, kingdom money is about to change hands. There is a divine force, a divine strength, a divine power, a divine might, a divine wisdom that is upon Zion that Deuteronomy 8:18 speaks about. There is also a divine sound that is coming from Zion that is saying I am about beautifying Zion, for her set time has come. Nothing or no one will be able to stop this season of divine and supernatural financial transaction and transition.

Let's go to the beginning to see God's response to the curse that affects his work.

Genesis 3:15, "And I will put enmity between thee and the woman, and between thy seed and her seed; it shall bruise thy head, and thou shalt bruise his heel."

In previous verses in Genesis we see where satan attacks God's handiwork, His best work man, and allow them to come under a curse by disobeying God. God responded to the curse, not just by talking, but this is what he said I will prepare myself a seed and that seed will take care of my need. That is exactly what God was saying in Genesis 33:15, "when he said, and I will put enmity between thee and the woman, and between thy seed and her seed; it shall bruise thy head, and thou shalt bruise his heel."

Galatians 3:13 -14, "Christ hath redeemed us from the curse of the law, being made a curse for us: for it is written, Cursed is everyone that hangeth on a tree: that the blessing of Abraham might come on the Gentiles through Jesus Christ; that we might receive the promise of the spirit through faith."

God's answer to the curse was the seed (offering), Jesus Christ. One of the reasons why God sowed that seed (offering) Jesus Christ to redeem us from the curse is that He wants the blessing of Abraham to come upon us.

John 3:16, "For God so loved the world that He gave his only begotten Son, that whosoever believeth in Him should not perish, but have everlasting life.

Here we see that because God so loved the world that He gave. As a Christian the only true proof that you love the world is when you are willing to give something that is significant to save it and change it. God sows the seed (offering) Jesus Christ and break curse. You can do the same also.

1John 3:8, "for this purpose the Son of God was manifested, that he might destroy the works of the devil."

Jesus Christ the seed, the offering was manifested to destroy the works of the devil. The curse of poverty is one of the works of the devil that Jesus came to deal with and he has dealt with it successfully.

God's answer to the curse is an offering. God lead the way and he expects us to do the same. As we move unto the next chapter we will study the offering that breaks the curse.

CHAPTER FIVE

THE OFFERING THAT BREAKS THE CURSE

We are going to look at offerings that were given and how the curse was broken. Before we go any future remember a curse can be anything that causes you lost, stops or hinder your progress.

I believe that in every child of God life there is an offering. When I say this, is it offering, I am talking about the offering that brings you out for good. In other words you will change financial lane, you will move out from the slow lane and get into the financial fast lane. On the financial slow lane money does not flow as it should. But on the financial fast lane money keep flowing and your possession growing. There is and offering that stops the keep curse. There is an offering that build a financial hedge around you. There is an offering that releases a multiplication, press down, shaken together and running over grace upon you. There is an offering that command heaven attention towards you. There is an offering that when it hits the earth it changes everything in the earth for your Good.

It is possible to give offerings all your life and remain poor all your life, and even die poor. Listen to me my brothers and sisters there is an offering that breaks the curse for good in your life. There is a thing like a change offering. The day is going to come if you listen to what I am telling you by the spirit of God, the Lord is going to tell you to give an offering that will require a step of faith, but it will also be a step into your financial future. God is saying to his people in this hour, give the offering that I have given to you to break the curse.

When we read the Old-Testament we see God dealt with curses by requesting that the children of Israel bring different kinds of offerings to deal with the curse. But it did not change the situation. They kept coming over and over again. Because the curse was not broken it was treated but not broken. This is why as a child of God you can experience a financial breakthrough today and pay some bills, but next week you need another breakthrough and on and on this keep happening in most of God's people life.

That is not what God is talking about when He wrote in His word about His people being wealthy. Let's go back to the offering that they presented to the Lord in the Old-Testament. Year after year they will kill animals until one day something changes when the offering change, let us look at John three sixteen.

John 3:16, "For God so love the world that He gave his only begotten."

It was that offering, His only Begotten Son that broke the curse.

Think about this, God is God but He needed an offering that cost Him something to deal with the curse. It is going to cost you if you want to break the curse. A curse is a spiritual force that affects the natural world that can only be broken after something is done in the natural and a supernatural reaction or response from heaven takes place. Something supernatural happens when you release the offering that breaks the curse. From the time the offering that breaks the curse is release in the earth something from heaven is released. We talk a lot about master keys that can open several doors but there is an offering that is call the master seed that breaks the curse and open extraordinary doors for you. When this seed is sown as God instructs you to, that is it, and financial freedom is yours for life. That seed (offering) will bring you under God financial care system. In other words you are covered for life under God financial system. When the financial door is open, consistency in the area of giving is necessary to keep finances flowing.

Galatians 3:13-14, "Christ hath redeemed us from the curse of the law, being made a curse for: for it is written, cursed is every one that hangeth on a tree: That the blessing of Abraham might come on the Gentiles through Jesus Christ; that we might receive the promise of the Spirit through faith."

Christ is that seed, He is the seed that took care of the curse of sin, sickness and poverty. When we look at verse (13) it says that Christ hath redeemed us from the curse. The seed was the remedy for the curse. Your seed, that special, unique, God inspire spirit led seed, when you sow it, the curse will be broken. Verse (14) says that the blessing of Abraham might come on the Gentiles (you and me). Please note the curse had to be dealt with in verse (13) before the blessing could take effect in verse (14). That is one of the reason why the Lord wants us to break the curse of poverty by giving that seed that breaks the curse. God wants the blessing to come upon you, do you want it.

1John 3:8 , "For this purpose the son of God was manifested, that he might destroy the works of the devil."

Jesus the Son of God was manifested to destroy the works of the devil. Poverty is one of the works of devil and Jesus the seed (offering) that break the curse. It is time that your seed that breaks the curse manifest itself and be sown and destroys the work of the devil of lack, need and poverty from working in your life. Whenever the offering that breaks the curse is manifested and sown in the God ordain soil it releases divine and supernatural financial provision. The offering that breaks the curse is not like any offering you have sown. God wrapped Himself (the anointing) in that seed that when it hit the soil it will spoil everything that needs to be spoiled. That offering has a divine seal upon it, it has resurrection power in it that everything, anything that belongs to you that has been dead, like a business, building projects, a dream and the list can go on and on will come back to life.

Another thing about the offering that breaks the curse, once it is sown, every other seed you sow after that, and your harvest will start accelerating. Money begins to move towards you, favor and opportunity like you have never seen before will start to flow.

2 Corinthians 8:9, "For ye know the grace of our Lord Jesus Christ, that, though he was rich, yet for your sakes he became poor, that ye through his poverty might be rich."

We saw in the word of God that Jesus Christ, the offering that breaks the curse became poor that we might become rich. The offering that breaks the curse got to be rich if it has to break the curse, it has to have some weight in the natural world in order to attract divine attention in the spirit world.

We have looked at what God did when he wanted to break the curse in the earth; he gave a precious, valuable and costly offering. As we have seen God lead by example by showing us what to do about the curse. We are going to look at the David now.

2 Samuel 24:17-25, "And David spake unto Lord when he saw the angel that smote the people, and said, Lo, I have

sinned, and I have done wickedly: but these sheep, what have they done? Let thine hand, I pray thee, be against me, and against my father's house. And Gad came that day to David, and said unto him, go up, rear an altar unto the Lord in the threshing-floor of Araunah the Jebusite. And David, according to the saying of Gad, went up as the Lord commanded. And Araunah looked, and saw the king and his servants coming on toward him: and Araunah went out, and bowed himself before the king on his face upon the ground. And Araunah said, wherefore is my Lord the king come to his servant?

And David said, to buy the threshing-floor of thee, to build an altar unto the Lord, that the plague may be stayed from the people. And Araunah said unto David, let my lord the king take an offering up what seemeth good unto him: behold here be oxen for burnt sacrifice, and the threshing instruments and other instruments of the oxen wood. All these things did Araunah, as a king, give unto the king. Araunah said unto the king, the Lord thy God accept thee. And the king said unto Araunah, nay; but I will surely buy it of thee at a price: neither will offer burnt offering unto the Lord my God of that which cost me nothing. So David bought the threshing- floor and the oxen for fifty shekels of sliver. And David built there an altar unto the Lord, and offered burnt offerings and peace offerings. So the Lord was entreated for the land, and the plague was stayed from Israel.

Verse fifteen (v.15) of the above chapter state that seventy thousand men, was lost because a curse hit the land. Are you tired of the curse, are you willing to do something about the curse, I hope your answer is yes. The curse is responsible for many lost opportunities and loses in your life. King David could not have taken it any more so he went to God about the curse and God in return when to the man of God and the man of God went to David. God will send a man of God your way, if you heed him something is going to happen for your good. Gad came to David in verse eighteen (v.18) and tell him to prepare and alter, in other words get ready to give an offering that breaks the curse.

In verse nineteen (v.19), we see David obey the word of the Lord that came to him through the man of God. The Bible says and David, according to the saying of Gad, went up as he was commanded. In verse twenty (v.20) he went to get his offering and he said what was the purpose of his offering to break the curse. In verse twenty- three (v.23) Araunah told David he will give him the sacrifice. In verse twenty- four (v.24) we see David refuse it; he said I will pay a price. You must pay the price and give the offering that breaks the curse. The seed that breaks the curse have to worth something of substance; it has to cost you something. The offering that breaks the curse in not an ordinary offering, it is not an average offering, it is an offering that will leave money stretch marks on you, in other words you will have to stretch financially to give this offering. In verse twenty- five (v.25) the Bible says after David offer up the offering that breaks the curse, God responded and the plague stayed away. There is an offering when sown it will keep poverty, lack, need, shortage off your life forever. And that is the offering I am talking about when I speak about the offering that breaks the curse. There is something in your hand when it is release it places a demand on heavens supply.

Saints of God, train your spirit to know the voice of God in the area of giving and listen for his voice. He will tell you the amount the offering that breaks the curse should be and where you should sow it, so that He can grow it.

There are some things that will never change in your life for good until you release the offering that breaks the curse.

CHAPTER SIX

YES, YOU CAN BREAK THE CURSE

I want you to know, it does not matter where you are in life financially there in an anointing that breaks financial yoke. There is an anointing that takes care of financial stroke. When I use the term financial stroke, I am referring to financial circumstances that seem that it would not move.

My personal Testimony

If anybody knows about the offering that breaks the curse is me. I am a living testimony that there is a seed that breaks the curse. Yes there is an offering that breaks the financial curse. I was a young man when I accepted the Lord. I accepted the Lord at age nineteen (19) I was not consistent with paying tithes and giving offerings. Until one day the Lord said to me, son I will not be able to bless you the way I want to if you do not pay tithes and give offerings. At this point in my life I was just working for three dollars an hour. I started paying tithes and giving small offerings because I did not have the knowledge that I have now about sowing and reaping. Although I was giving I was not receiving as I would like to.

One day while I was changing my clothes to go to church the Lord spoke to me, He said Dexter there is anointing to prosper in the natural, look at Abraham, Isaac, Joseph and the three Hebrews boys they prospered in the natural. I started reading the word of God and I started to learn about sowing and reaping. Also I starting listening to other preachers, preach on the subject. This is about five years after.

I started sowing more and receiving more I was even promote on my job several times but I was not free financially. I was still having financial challenges the curse was being treated but not broken. In October 2007 the month of our church anniversary (Warriors assembly C.O.G.O.P) I committed ten thousand dollars ($10000.00) to it. And that was my, this is it offering, my financial situation have never been the same, as I am writing this book I am loaded compare to where I was years ago. I started reaping the next month (November) a pastor call me and ask me to come and see him, at my arrival he said he was praying about a need that he had and also about a seed to sow and my name came up, the Lord told him Dexter and he wrote a cheque for me for ten thousand dollars **($10,000.00)** and lots of money kept flowing after that day. I have received lots of ten thousand from other people and above in one gift, I receive a sixty five thousand dollars **($65,000.00)** gift one time. Let me give you two ten thousand dollars **(10,000.00)** testimony now. I was preaching in one of my covenant wealth meeting and I was prompted by the Lord to give a prophet one thousand dollars **($1000.00).** After I did that a woman told me while I was still preaching that Lord spoke to her to give me ten thousand dollars **($10,000.00)** I collected it the same night. I was in another meeting and while preaching a couple walked up to me and gave me and envelope, when I open it, there was ten thousand dollars **($10000.00)** in it. I am financially blessed I have everything that a human being need naturally to be comfortable. And I continue to sow (give) large sums of money into the kingdom of God and also bless others.

This is why I wrote this chapter and give it this title; yes you can break the curse. Saints of God, I know by experience I am walking in a financial anointing that cannot be stopped or denied because I am connected to Adoni, I walk in a financial grace that I will always win the financial race.

I do not know the offering that will break the financial curse for you. It might be less than ten thousand ($10,000) or more than ten thousand ($10,000). Just listen to God and He will tell you because He wants you free financially.

I hope this book has been a blessing to you. If you have not yet received Jesus as your Saviour do so now by saying this simple prayer.

Lord Jesus I come to you forgive of my sins save me and I will live for you.

Should you believe God is leading you to ***Warriors Assembly Growing Church Breakthrough Ministries***, here are our current locations:

1. Princes Town (Restoration City)

Bless Avenue, New Grant, Princess Town
1 (868) 347-7180, 494-4604

2. Couva (Head Quarters)
147 Southern Main Road
1 (868) 289-4325, 388-2769

3. Aripero (House of Prophetic Destiny)
1414 Aripero Village, Rousillac
(Deo's Shopping Mall) 1 (868) 752-0056

4. Siparia (House of Power)
15 High Street (Upstairs KFC)
1 (868) 491-7153

5. Arouca (House of Uncommon Wisdom)
11 Eastern Main Road, (Upstairs BJ's Drug World)
Five Rivers 1 (868) 289-4325

***Chaguanas (Winner's Chapel)**
2nd Floor, Regency Business Centre
Cnr Penco & Gaston Streets
1 (868) 289-4325

Made in the USA
Monee, IL
04 November 2026

67380042R00022